700029734383

D0312116

Tudor
Britain

Stewart Ross

W

FRANKLIN WATTS
LONDON • SYDNEY

BUILDING STYLES

Tudor Britain was a land of few people and mile after mile of farmland, woodland and hillside. Some ninety percent of the population made their living from agriculture, dwelling in small villages or isolated farms. Most remaining 16th-century homes, therefore, can be seen outside large towns.

Wooden frames

Most remaining Tudor buildings are known as 'half-timbered'. A glance at the picture (below) will show you why. Houses like this were built where strong wood, like oak, was readily available. The timber frame was put together first. The beams were joined with wooden pegs. Then a roof of thatch or tiles was placed on top.

Wattle and daub

The gaps between the timber beams were filled with either brick or wattle and daub. Wattles were thin sticks of wood. Daub was the mud or plaster pasted over them. When the beams are stained black and the filling painted white, these houses are known as 'black-and-white'.

PAST TO PRESENT

Houses have been roofed with a thatch of straw or reeds for thousands of years. The length of time a thatched roof lasts depends on the quality of the materials as well as the workmanship. Well-made thatch may last fifty years. It is still used today in traditional housing. Not only does it look good, it also provides excellent insulation. Thatched roofs were popular with the Tudors, too. This cottage near Stratford-upon-Avon was the home of Anne Hathaway. She was the wife of the famous playwright William Shakespeare.

The Tudors did not suddenly introduce a new style of building. This house in Pembridge, Herefordshire, for instance, has a Tudor addition (left) built on to a slightly older medieval house (right).

Local materials

Transporting heavy materials like wood, brick and stone was extremely costly in Tudor times. As a result, most people built their homes using local materials. For example, cottages in north Wales were constructed of stone and roofed with slate found nearby. In some areas of England, builders used local stone both for the walls and the roof tiles.

This house in Lewes, Sussex, was given to King Henry VIII's fourth wife, Anne of Cleves, after their divorce. The walls were built using pieces of flint found in the surrounding chalk hills. It is now a museum.

The decorated tiles on the first floor were made from clay dug from a nearby estuary.

THE MANOR HOUSE

Across the country a small number of 16th-century manor houses still stand. These houses – bigger than cottages but not mansions – were built by successful men. Some had made their fortunes from politics, some from trade or commerce, and some from farming.

Building in peaceful times

Unlike earlier manor houses, Tudor ones were not built to be defended from attack. This was partly because Tudor Britain was relatively peaceful, and partly because there was little point in making a house defensible since Tudor cannons were powerful enough to destroy stone and brick walls.

The top of the tower of Ingatestone Hall looks like one on a medieval castle, but it is just for decoration. The step effect on the wall at the front of the house is a typical Tudor feature, similar to the one on Plas Mawr in Conwy (see page 16).

Pipes and drains

Ingatestone Hall (above) has an interesting history. When King Henry VIII ordered the destruction of nearby Barking Abbey in 1539 he gave much of the monastery's wealth to his servant, William Petre. Petre used his new-found riches to build a splendid new manor house for himself and his family. Ingatestone was one of the first private houses in Britain since Roman times to have piped water and drains. There were no flushing toilets in Tudor times, only wooden buckets or seats overhanging the walls!

From this small building in the grounds, water was piped to Ingatestone Hall.

Fashionable manors

Tudor Manor houses came in all shapes and sizes. Rich landowners built long, narrow rooms called galleries in their houses where ladies and gentlemen could exercise under cover or even dance. John Moreton added a fashionable long gallery (below) to his black-and-white manor house Little Moreton Hall in Cheshire.

FANTASTIC CHIMNEYS

In the Middle Ages people burned wood on their fires. In smaller houses the smoke had to find its own way out through a hole in the roof. In Tudor times coal was becoming popular, so homes needed proper fireplaces and chimneys to let out the thick, black coal smoke. The Tudors loved their chimneys, often giving them fantastic shapes like these on Hampton Court, Surrey.

This Long Gallery was added to Little Moreton Hall in the late 16th century, but its weight caused the whole building to sag out of shape.

Mansions

In Tudor Britain an enormous gulf separated the very wealthy and powerful from the poor. The few really rich people lived in staggering splendour. A number of their houses remain. Each one, with its vast grounds and dozens of rooms, was almost as large as a small town.

Elizabethan glory

Burghley House (above) was built by Queen Elizabeth I's advisor, William Cecil, Lord Burghley. This huge and elaborately decorated mansion shows how wealthy Lord Burghley was. Its design was the height of fashion in Elizabethan times, when a passion for building in the Renaissance style was sweeping Britain. This new approach, which began in Italy, was heavily influenced by the architecture of ancient Greece and Rome. Renaissance influence is seen in the straight lines of Burghley House, and the domes and columns of its roof.

Built in the late Tudor period, Burghley House, Lincolnshire, shows the influence of Renaissance styles imported from Italy. These domes, for instance, are like those found on Italian churches. The wall ornament (inset, top) was also influenced by fashionable Italian style.

The windows on the upper floors of Hardwick Hall are larger than those at the bottom. This is because the owner did not want to spend money on large, expensive windows for the rooms where servants lived.

SEE FOR YOURSELF
Here are some of the Tudor mansions that remain to this day.
1 Gwydir Castle, Conwy
2 Hardwick Hall, Derbyshire
3 Burghley House, Lincolnshire
4 Melford Hall, Suffolk
5 Kentwell Manor, Suffolk
6 Layer Marney Tower, Essex
7 Compton Wynyates, Warwickshire

Walls of glass

Hardwick Hall, Derbyshire (above) was built by Elizabeth, Countess of Shrewsbury, in late Tudor times. Its windows fill the walls. Workmen were not able to make large sheets of clear, flat glass, so windows were made up of many smaller panes held together by strips of lead.

Glass was expensive and had been widely used in domestic windows for only around 100 years. This meant the Countess of Shrewsbury's design showed her wealth and high position in society. The windows of ordinary homes were closed with wooden shutters or even pieces of leather.

False start

Layer Marney Tower (right) is the grandest gatehouse in England, built by the Marney family early in King Henry VIII's reign. Lord Henry Marney, Captain of the King's Bodyguard, wanted to outdo other noblemen by building a vast palace. Unfortunately he and his son died after only the tower and a few other buildings had been finished. They left no children, so the rest of the palace remained unbuilt.

What is now called Layer Marney Tower was originally built as a gatehouse, or entrance, to an even larger house that was never completed. A gatehouse protected the entrance to a courtyard, and this one is designed to look rather like a medieval castle.

11

ROYAL RESIDENCES

The English and Scottish rulers of Tudor times had several homes and they rarely stayed in the same one for long. Queen Elizabeth I of England, for example, moved between Windsor Castle, the Tower of London, Hampton Court and other palaces near London. She also stayed in rich people's homes.

Whose court?

Lord Chancellor Wolsey built Hampton Court, Surrey (right) for himself but three years later he gave it to King Henry VIII as a way to gain favour. Notice from the photo how battlements (the low walls at the roof level) are now used simply as decoration, not for defence as they were in medieval times. The royal coat of arms, which was added when the Court became the King's, is clearly visible above the arch. So is the fine projecting window, known as an oriel. Oriel windows looked attractive from the outside and gave people inside a wider view as they looked out on the world.

The grand entrance to Hampton Court, Surrey, showed all who entered that its builder, Cardinal Wolsey, was second only to the king in importance.

12

Built in 1503 by Mary Queen of Scots' grandfather, James IV, the Great Hall of Stirling Castle in Scotland was designed so that all the important members of the royal court could gather and feast together. Today, 500 years later, guests still meet and dine beneath its splendid timber roof. This style of roof, in which beams are supported on others projecting from the walls, is known as a 'hammer-beam' roof.

Holyroodhouse, Edinburgh, Scotland, was built in the early Tudor period. The massive round towers show that the Scots continued to build castle-style buildings at a time when they were going out of fashion in England.

A Scottish palace

The palace of Holyroodhouse, Edinburgh (above) was begun by King James IV of Scotland in about 1500 and altered by his son, James V, who added the large windows in the towers. At that time Scotland was peaceful so Holyroodhouse was not built to be defended. King James V's daughter, Mary Queen of Scots, spent much of her reign at Holyroodhouse.

IN THE KITCHEN

The Tudor kitchens that survive belonged to the larger houses of the well-to-do. A grand household could make just about everything it needed – from bread to beer – from the basic ingredients produced on its own land. Also, because everything had to be done by hand, preparing food for a large household was labour-intensive.

Food was cooked on an open fire. To the left of the fire is a copper basin with a fire beneath it for producing hot water for washing.

A farmer's kitchen

We know what Tudor kitchens were like from examining remaining Tudor kitchens and researching written records that have survived from Tudor times. The pictures here are all of the reconstructed Winkhurst Tudor kitchen at the Weald & Downland Museum, Sussex. The family that lived here would have been of the yeoman class – they were independent farmers who lived comfortably off their own land. Much of the work in the kitchen would have been done by servants supervised by the mistress of the household.

At work in a Tudor kitchen: with all that wood about, candles were always a dangerous form of lighting. The wooden tub on the table at the right is for making butter.

Storing and cooking food

The materials the Tudors used – wood, iron, copper, brass and pottery – are very different from those in a modern kitchen. There are no plastics, steel or aluminium. There is no sink or running water. Water came in a wooden bucket from the well outside. There's no fridge, either, because electric power was not available in Tudor times. Food lasted more than a few days only if it was salted, smoked, dried or pickled. It was stored in tubs, baskets or pottery jars, many of which still survive today. Fire was the only means of cooking and heating, and wood from the surrounding area was used as fuel.

A dome-shaped clay oven for baking bread, heated by a wood fire lit beneath it. Every Tudor household baked its own bread.

Most Tudor storage vessels were pottery jars. They were covered with cloth or wooden lids to keep out flies and mice.

TOWN HOUSES

Towns, the centres of business and trade, grew swiftly in Tudor times. Even so, apart from London, Norwich, Bristol and York, they all had less than 10,000 inhabitants. London, with perhaps 200,000 citizens, was by far the largest city. Sadly, because almost all Tudor town houses were made of wood, many of London's were lost in the Great Fire of 1666.

Gem in the high street

The finest Tudor town house still standing is in the high street in Conwy, north Wales (right). Named Plas Mawr (Great Hall), it was built for the merchant Robert Wynn at the end of the 16th century. Note the impressive entrance and the broad windows with small leaded panes of glass. These features are a sign of their owner's wealth and status.

Inside and out

Private bedrooms, like the one where William Shakespeare may have been born in Stratford-upon-Avon (below), were a Tudor development. They gave the householder privacy impossible in earlier times. Curtains around four-poster beds kept in the warmth and shut out cold draughts.

Robert Wynn built Plas Mawr in the centre of Conwy, Wales, so his friends and neighbours were left in no doubt about his success in business. The triangle-shaped stone decoration above the windows reflects the architecture of ancient Greece and Rome — a sure sign of the influence of the Renaissance.

This bedroom in Stratford-upon-Avon where Shakespeare may have been born in 1564 has been decorated in Tudor style. People who could not afford to hang expensive tapestries often painted the walls, as here, with tapestry-like designs.

The top two storeys of this half-timbered town house in Canterbury, Kent (below), are larger than the ground floor, so they jut out over the street. This was done to get the maximum floor space on a small building plot.

SEE FOR YOURSELF

Here are a few of the Tudor town houses that you can visit today.
1 Plas Mawr, Conwy
2 Tudor Merchant's House, Tenby
3 Sutton House, Hackney, London

You can also see Tudor town houses in Stratford-upon-Avon (4), Burford (5) and Lavenham (6).

Since wood was widely used in the construction of Tudor houses, carving was one of the most popular forms of decoration. Projecting beams and exposed timber were often carved with all kinds of designs, like these flowers on a house in Canterbury, Kent. The detail in the woodwork below can be seen just above the ground floor windows.

A Commercial People

In Tudor times the discovery of other continents opened up business opportunities for merchants and adventurers. At the same time the population rose, so more food, cloth and other materials were needed. Evidence of the boom in trade and commerce can be found in many Tudor buildings.

This Tudor shop in Lavenham, Suffolk does not appear to be standing on very secure foundations. Also note the overhanging upper floor and the arch over the door. Both features are typical of Tudor buildings.

Shops as workplaces

The picture on the right is of a Tudor shop front. The hinged boards had a double function: they covered the windows at night and during the day they swung out to act as a display counter. The wares on sale were made by a craftsman and his apprentices at the back of the building.

Shopping under shelter

Some rich people liked to show they were thinking of those less fortunate than themselves. For instance, in 1501 Bishop Story of Chichester paid for a market (opposite page, top) in the centre of the town to give shelter to local traders. Some market shelters were paid for by groups of master craftsmen, known as guilds. The halls they built – guildhalls – also served as meeting places for guild members.

The stone market, where four roads meet at the centre of Chichester, Sussex, is based upon the complicated design for the buttresses that supported the walls of cathedrals. The very top was added after Tudor times.

The covered market at Pembridge, Herefordshire (below), was built by local business people. Its eight carved oak posts originally supported an upper storey, which no longer survives. Unlike the bishop of Chichester's stone market shelter, it is built in wood, which was much cheaper.

The Tudor covered market in the village of Pembridge, Herefordshire (right) is much simpler in style. It still stands in the old market place, next to a Tudor inn.

Inns and travellers

Ale sold at inns was made on the premises. This meant the beer in every pub was different. There were inns all over Tudor England because travel by horse or on foot was slow, so plenty of stopping places were needed not too far apart.

Although England and Wales were more peaceful in Tudor times, the country faced threats from abroad. Tudor monarchs successfully protected their kingdom from attack by other countries.

By 1539 the rulers of the Catholic countries of Europe were unhappy with England's King Henry VIII for rejecting the Roman Catholic Church and setting up the Church of England in its place. The king feared his country might be invaded by France and responded by building a huge chain of forts along the south coast. As at Calshot Castle (below), Tudor fort design included gun mountings and rounded walls to deflect enemy cannon balls.

SEE FOR YOURSELF
Here are some of Henry VIII's coastal forts that can still be seen.
1. Derby Fort, Isle of Man
2. Pendennis Castle, Cornwall
3. St Mawes Castle, Cornwall
4. Yarmouth Castle, Isle of Wight
5. Calshot Castle, Hampshire
6. Southsea Castle, Hampshire
7. Camber Castle, East Sussex
8. Dover Castle, Kent
9. Walmer Castle, Kent
10. Deal Castle, Kent

Henry VIII built Calshot Castle to defend the port of Southampton from French attack. The walls were flat-topped, so cannons could be placed there.

Scottish or English?
During the 16th century, England and Scotland were independent countries, governed entirely separately. Although there were marriage links between the Tudors and the Stuart rulers of Scotland, there was frequent fighting between the two nations. Fortifications in northern England and southern Scotland remain from this conflict.

In 1558 Queen Elizabeth I began rebuilding the defences of the border town of Berwick-upon-Tweed (right) at the enormous cost (for those days) of £250,000. This tells us how important Berwick was and how keen the new queen was to keep out the Scots. The style of the fortifications is unusual, too. Instead of the tall stone walls of a medieval castle, Berwick's walls are low, thick and earth-filled. This allowed them to withstand cannon fire that would smash a traditional wall to smithereens.

A Scottish home

John Strachan was obviously not thinking of resisting cannon when he built Claypots Castle (below) in the late 16th century. Even so, this extraordinary-looking building near Dundee in Scotland was capable of holding out against lightly-armed attackers. Claypots is evidence that life in Scotland was not yet as peaceful as neighbouring England.

Scotsgate (above) was the main entrance into Berwick-upon-Tweed, the only town in England surrounded by Elizabethan walls. The picture shows the thickness of the walls, necessary to withstand cannon fire.

Cumberland Bastion, Berwick (above), is one of five strong points placed around the city walls. It was built according to the latest Italian wall design and relied not upon the height of its walls but upon their massive earth-filled thickness.

Claypots Castle is unique. The architect kept the traditional Scottish round tower design, then placed square living quarters on the top. As a result, the lower rooms have curved walls while the upper ones are straight.

SCHOOLS

The Tudors also built many new schools. More schools survive from Tudor times than from all the previous centuries. During the Tudor period education was much in demand, and the number of people who could read rose significantly. Some boys studied in parish schools that operated in their local church or in the schoolmaster's own home. There were no schools for girls in Tudor times.

Education for local boys

When the wealthy cloth merchant John Cooke, Mayor of Gloucester, wanted to do something for his community, he built a school (below) for local boys. In 1539 Cooke's widow, Joan, gave the school to the city of Gloucester. Inside there was originally one large hall where the whole school sat on benches listening to the words of the schoolmaster.

John Cooke, the proud builder of St Mary de Crypt Grammar School, made sure that he would be remembered by having his coat of arms carved on the outside of the school building.

The splendid building that was once St Mary de Crypt Grammar School still stands in the centre of Gloucester, with its coat of arms and oriel window (see page 12). The front of the building – the part that visitors see first – is faced with expensive stone. Round the back the walls are just plain brick.

Schools for priests

At about the same time, William of Waynflete, Bishop of Winchester, wanted bright students for Magdalen College, Oxford, which he had recently founded to train priests. He set up several grammar schools, one of which was Magdalen College School in his home town of Wainfleet (right). (Grammar schools were so called because they taught Latin grammar.) It was brick-built in the latest fashion with expensive stained glass in the windows.

Brick had been used in Roman times but during the medieval period wood and stone were the main building materials. By the late 15th century, when Magdalen College School (above), was built, brick was being used more and more.

Berkhamsted School, Hertfordshire (left), was built to educate the sons of local gentry, farmers and business people. Covering such a wide space tested 16th-century builders to the limit and required huge wooden beams expertly placed to take the weight of the roof.

King's schools

When Henry VIII and his son Edward VI broke up the Roman Catholic Church in England, many church schools were replaced with new schools named after the king. In just one year, 1541, Henry VIII refounded seven new schools in his own name.

UNIVERSITIES AND CHARITIES

Oxford and Cambridge, England's only universities in Tudor times, had been set up largely to train young men to become priests. Rich individuals believed it was their duty to pay for the building and running of university colleges. Many of these fine buildings are still with us.

Chapels and halls

In some ways these colleges were like monasteries. The largest and most impressive buildings were the chapels and the halls where the students ate together. At the centre of each college was an open space, as below at the University of St Andrew's in Scotland. This was like the cloister where monks walked.

The University of St Andrew's in Fife, Scotland, is the third oldest university in Britain, founded in the early 15th century. St Mary's College (below) was built in the 1530s and is still the centre for religious studies at St Andrew's.

Built over a period of 150 years, the chapel at King's College, Cambridge, was not finished until the reign of Henry VIII. The glorious fan-vaulted roof is among Europe's finest examples of medieval-style architecture. Its date is confirmed by the huge Tudor roses carved in stone.

PAST TO PRESENT

When Sir John Boys paid for his 'hospital' (house for the poor) in Canterbury in 1595, he had a plaque carved to remind inmates of his charity: 'SIR IHON BOYS KNIGHT FOUNDED THIS HOSPITALL ANNO (in the year of) 1595'. Remarkably, thanks to the addition of piped water, drains and electricity, Boys' buildings are still lived in today.

Hospitals for the poor

Wealthy Tudors built hundreds of dwellings or resting places for the elderly poor. They called them 'hospitals' or 'alms-houses'. The entrances were often impressive in order to reflect the importance of the person who had paid for them. The accommodation was generally in dormitories and meals were eaten in common dining rooms. Kitchens and wash blocks were at the back.

CHURCHES AND RELIGION

Religious quarrels in Tudor Britain led to many changes in the way people worshipped. Henry VIII separated England and Wales from the Roman Catholic Church. From the 1530s onwards many people died for their beliefs and church building stopped. Monasteries were destroyed and the interiors of churches were stripped of signs of Catholicism.

Although it was built in Tudor times, Lavenham church was built in the medieval Perpendicular style of architecture, which was noted for its flat arches and battlement decorations.

Still building

At the beginning of the Tudor age churches were still being built or re-built all over the land. A great tower, known as 'Bell Harry', was added to Canterbury Cathedral. At Lavenham, Suffolk, cloth merchants clubbed together to build an entirely new church (right). Construction started in 1486 and the church was finished 30 years later.

Closing the monasteries

Britain is dotted with the ruins of medieval monasteries and nunneries. Many had been among the most noble buildings in the country. To Henry VIII, though, they were a tempting source of wealth and he closed them down and seized their precious contents. Most of these buildings soon became sad ruins.

Destruction in churches

In Edward VI's reign (1547–1553) other signs of Catholicism were destroyed. Protestants (religious reformers) did not accept that the mass should be a mystery. Screens that prevented the congregation from seeing the service of mass taking place were removed. Keen Protestants also believed that all religious images of people were against God's law and so destroyed thousands of church statues, paintings and stained glass windows.

PRIEST HOLES

Very early in Elizabeth I's reign (1558–1603), England was officially a Protestant country. Later, Catholic priests entered the country in secret to convert the people back to Catholicism. When danger lurked, they hid in priest holes tucked away in the corners of stately homes owned by Catholics. The hole was a small, specially-made hiding place, often under the floor or between the walls.

The brilliantly painted screen (left) at Attleborough, Norfolk was saved from Protestants only because parishioners dismantled it and hid it away. The church's medieval wall paintings (above) were badly damaged.

ENTERTAINMENT

For most of their entertainments the Tudors did not need special buildings. Their rough-and-ready football had no stadiums, and their processions and carnivals took place in the street. There were inns, where they might enjoy a mug of ale and conversation, and there were shoddily-built rings where cock fighting and other cruel sports took place.

The Middle Temple Hall, Blackfriars, London, was where lawyers were (and still are) dined and entertained. The amazing Tudor roof is a double hammer beam. The roof timbers rest on projecting beams that themselves rest on other beams sticking out from the walls.

Halls and inns

The first plays were performed in squares and streets. By early in Elizabeth I's reign actors also used the courtyards of coaching inns. Large halls, such as Middle Temple Hall (right), were also used to stage plays.

Several of William Shakespeare's plays were performed for the monarch in the royal palaces of Hampton Court, Whitehall and Richmond where there were halls big enough to hold a stage and a large number of spectators.

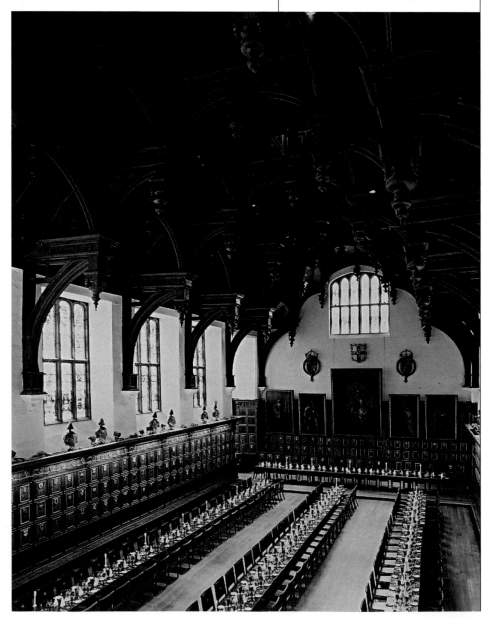

Shakespeare's Globe burned down in 1613. Sparks from a cannon, used for sound effects, set the thatched roof on fire. A replacement was quickly constructed, but that was eventually pulled down. Some 300 years later the American Sam Wanamaker set about rebuilding the original theatre as it had been in Shakespeare's day. It finally opened in 1997, giving us a chance to find out what one of the most remarkable buildings of the Tudor age was like.

The Globe Theatre, London, is a perfect copy of Shakespeare's theatre which burned down during the great playwright's lifetime.

Theatres

The first purpose-built theatre was built in London in 1577. It was a great success and soon several others were built. They were large, many-sided structures with the stage jutting forward into a courtyard in the middle. The courtyard was surrounded by galleries with wooden benches in them. The audience paid one penny to stand in the yard or more for a covered gallery seat. The most famous of these playhouses was the Globe (above and right, reconstructed), because it was where many of Shakespeare's plays were performed.

TIMELINE

1485	Henry Tudor defeats King Richard III at the Battle of Bosworth and becomes King Henry VII, the first of the Tudor monarchs.
1485–1509	Reign of Henry VII.
1509–1547	Reign of Henry VIII.
1534	Henry VIII quarrels with the Roman Catholic Pope and becomes head of the new Church of England. Protestant reforms are introduced.
1536	England and Wales are united.
1536–1540	Henry VIII shuts down Roman Catholic monasteries and nunneries and sells off their possessions.
1540s	Henry VIII and Edward VI found many new schools.
1547–1553	Reign of Edward VI. He supports Protestant reforms.
1553–1558	Reign of Mary I. She tries to bring back the Roman Catholic religion.
1558–1603	Reign of Elizabeth I.
1577–1580	Sir Francis Drake sails around the world.
1588	The English fleet defeats the invading Spanish Armada (fleet). William Shakespeare starts writing plays.
1598–1601	Parishes are made responsible for helping local poor people.
1599	The Globe Theatre opens in London.
1603	Elizabeth I dies. King James VI of Scotland becomes King James I of England and Wales, too.

GLOSSARY

alms help, usually money, given to the poor.

apprentice young person learning a trade from a master.

buttress a structure that projects from the wall of a building to support it.

cardinal one of the highest Roman Catholic priests, responsible for choosing the pope.

coat of arms a kind of badge of class allowed only to the families of gentlemen.

cock fighting sport in which cocks were fitted with spurs and encouraged to fight each other.

fresco painting done on wet plaster.

guildhall town assembly hall, usually for the leaders of local businesses.

half-timbered house built on a visible wooden frame.

hammer-beam type of roof in which the beams are arranged in steps up from the wall.

leaded glass small triangles of glass with lead between.

Lord Treasurer minister responsible for the kingdom's finances.

manor area of land supervised by a local lord.

mass a special religious service.

medieval of the Middle Ages (roughly 1066–1485).

mock-Tudor imitation Tudor.

monastery building in which monks live, work and pray.

pestle and mortar instrument for grinding food into powder, consisting of a dish (mortar) and a heavy stick (pestle).

plaque board or tablet to remember something.

Renaissance period of history (roughly 1350–1600) when Europeans showed a new interest in the ancient Greek and Roman civilisations.

vault large ceiling area, usually of stone.

PLACES TO VISIT

Britain has many Tudor houses and museums, some of which are listed here. Contact your local tourist board for information about places in your area.

Burghley House, Stamford, Lincolnshire
www.burghley.co.uk
England's largest Tudor stately home.

Eastbury Manor House, Barking, London
www.barking-dagenham.gov.uk
Elizabethan merchant's brick-built house.

Globe Theatre, Bankside, London
www.shakespeares-globe.org
Reconstructed Tudor theatre where Shakespeare's plays are performed.

Gwydir Castle, Conwy, Wales
www.gwydir-castle.co.uk
A stone-built courtyard house.

Hampton Court Palace, London
www.hrp.org.uk
Tudor royal palace with many displays about Tudor life.

Hardwick Hall, Chesterfield, Derbyshire
www.nationaltrust.org.uk
One of the best examples of a Tudor mansion.

Kentwell Manor, Long Melford, Suffolk
www.kentwell.co.uk
A Tudor house that is now a centre for re-enactment of life in Tudor times.

Little Moreton Hall, Congleton, Cheshire
www.nationaltrust.org.uk
Moated manor house with decorative timber framework and a magnificent long gallery.

Melford Hall, Sudbury, Suffolk
www.nationaltrust.org.uk
Brick Tudor mansion with a panelled banqueting hall where Elizabeth I was entertained.

Middle Temple Hall, Blackfriars, London
www.middletemple.org.uk
Brick common room for members of the Middle Temple Inn with a double hammer-beam roof and beautifully carved wooden screen.

Montacute House, Somerset
www.nationaltrust.org.uk
Elizabethan stone-built house with Renaissance-style chimneys, parapets and plasterwork.

Oxburgh Hall, King's Lynn, Norfolk
www.nationaltrust.org.uk
Brick-built early Tudor moated manor house with impressive gatehouse and a priest's hole.

Palace of Holyroodhouse, Edinburgh, Scotland
www.royal.gov.uk
A royal palace containing the apartments that Mary, Queen of Scots lived in.

Plas Mawr, Conwy, Wales
www.cadw.wales.gov.uk
Britain's finest surviving Elizabethan town house.

Rufford Old Hall, Ormskirk, Lancashire
www.nationaltrust.org.uk
Has a spectacular great hall with a dramatic hammer-beam roof.

Sutton House, Hackney, London
www.nationaltrust.org.uk
Tudor house with oak-panelled rooms.

Trerice, Newquay, Cornwall
www.nationaltrust.org.uk
Elizabethan manor house with a great chamber.

Tudor Merchant's House, Tenby, Wales
www.nationaltrust.org.uk
Stone house with paintings on the interior walls and a Flemish-style round chimney.

Weald & Downland Museum, Sussex
www.wealddown.co.uk
Includes the re-created Winkhurst Tudor kitchen and a Tudor market hall.

INDEX